ᐃᒃᐱᐊᕐᔪᖕᒥᐅᑕᐅᓪᓗᓂ ᖁᕕᐊᓇᖅᑐᖅ ᑲᔅᓵᖅᓇᖅᓯᓂᓗ

It Is Good to Live in Beautiful Arctic Bay

ᑎᑎᕋᖅᑐᖅ
ᓘᓯ ᖃᕙᕙᐅᖅ

ᑎᑎᖅᑐᓯᖅᑐᖅ
ᐊᒦᐅᓪ ᓵᓐᑦᓚᓐᑦ

WRITTEN BY
Lucy Qavavauq

ILLUSTRATED BY
Amiel Sandland

ᓂᑮᑕᐅᔪᖓ. ᐃᒃᐱᐊᕐᔪᖕᒥᐅᑕᐅᔪᖓ ᑲᔾᔮᕐᓇᖅᑐᐊᓗᖕᒥ, ᓄᓇᕗᒻᒥ.
My name is Nikita. I love to live in beautiful Arctic Bay, Nunavut.

ᐅᑭᐅᒃᑯᑦ ᐃᒃᐱᐊᕐᔪᖕᒥ ᑖᖓᒡᔪᐊᓲᖅ. ᑕᐃᒪᐃᑎᓪᓗᒍ ᑕᐃᔭᐅᓲᖅ "ᑕᐅᖓᒡᔪᐊᕐᒥ."
ᑕᐅᖓᒡᔪᐊᕋᓗᐊᖅᑎᓪᓗᒍ, ᐃᒃᐱᐊᕐᔪᒃ ᓱᓕ ᑲᔾᔮᕐᓇᖅᑐᖅ ᓄᓇᒋᓪᓗᒍ. ᐊᖅᓴᕐᓃᑦ ᑕᑯᒥᓇᖅᑐᐊᓘᓲᑦ ᑕᐃᒪᐃᓕᖅᑎᓪᓗᒍ ᐊᕐᕌᒍᒥ. ᐃᓄᐃᑦ ᑕᐅᑐᒃᑐᑦ ᐃᒪᐃᓕᓲᑦ, "ᐅᐊᒃ ᐱᐅᔪᑦ."
In Arctic Bay, part of the winter is always dark. This time is called "the great darkness."
But even in the great darkness, Arctic Bay is a beautiful place to live. The northern lights are amazing at this time of year. Watching them makes people say, "Wow. That's beautiful."

ᑕᐅᕙᒡᔪᐊᓚᐅᖅᑎᓪᓗᒍ, ᓯᕿᓂᖅ ᓴᖅᑭᑕᐃᓐᓇᕌᖓᑦ ᓄᓇᐅᑉ ᑭᒡᓕᓪᓗᐊᖓᒍᑦ ᓴᖅᑭᓵᖅ. ᐃᔨᑦᑕ ᐃᒡᓗᐊ ᓯᑯᙱᖅᓱᒍ ᖁᖓᕐᓱᑕ ᑐᙵᓱᒃᑎᓲᕗᑦ. ᑕᐃᒪᐃᓕᐅᓲᖑᔪᒍᑦ ᐅᑎᖅᑲᑦᑕᐃᓐᓇᕐᓂᐊᕐᒪᑦ. ᐅᖃᓲᖑᔪᒍᑦ, “ᑐᙵᓱᑎᑦ ᓯᕿᓃᖅ.”
After the great darkness, the sun finally rises over the horizon. We squint our eyes and smile with one side of our face to welcome it back. We do this so that it will keep coming back. We say, “Welcome, Sun.”

CTIC BAY
NAVUT

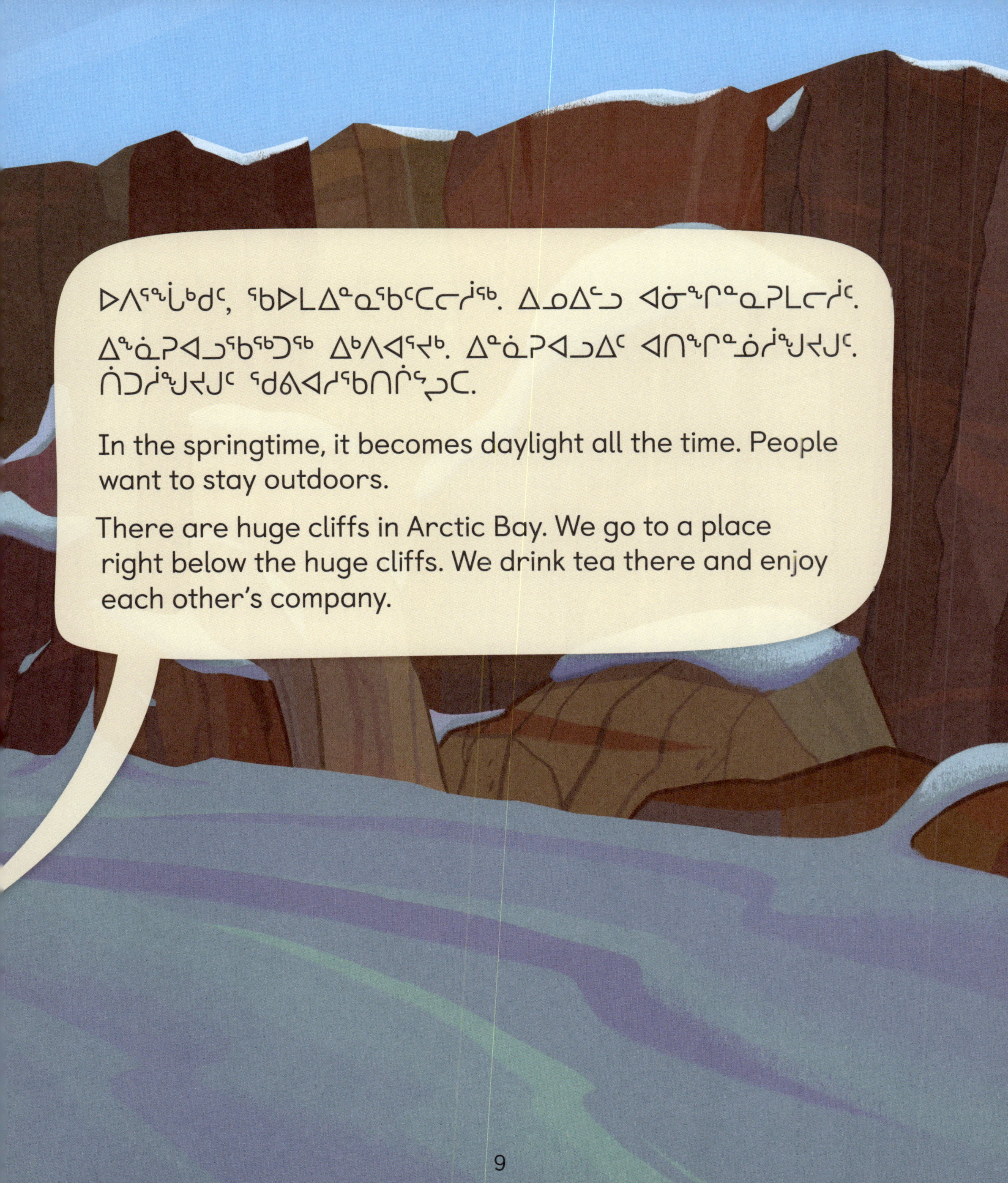
ᐅᐱᕐᖔᒃᑯᑦ, ᖃᐅᒪᐃᓐᓇᖅᑲᑦᑕᓕᓲᖅ. ᐃᓄᐃᑦᑐ ᐊᓃᖕᒋᓐᓇᕈᒪᓕᓲᑦ.
ᐃᖕᓈᕈᐊᓗᖅᑲᖅᑐᖅ ᐃᒃᐱᐊᕐᔪᒃ. ᐃᓐᓈᕈᐊᓗᐃᑦ ᐊᑎᖕᒋᓐᓅᓲᖑᔪᒍᑦ. ᑏᑐᓲᖑᔪᒍᑦ ᖁᕕᐊᓱᒃᑎᒌᖕᓗᑕ.
In the springtime, it becomes daylight all the time. People want to stay outdoors.
There are huge cliffs in Arctic Bay. We go to a place right below the huge cliffs. We drink tea there and enjoy each other's company.

ᐊᐅᓪᓛᓰᖑᕐᒥᔪᒍᑦ ᐅᐱᕐᖄᒃᑯᑦ. ᐃᓪᓗᑯᓗᒃᐸᑦ, ᐊᖑᑎᖃᑎᒌᑦ ᐊᕐᓇᖃᑎᒌᓪᓗ ᑲᑎᙵᕙᒃᑕᒌᑦ. ᑲᔾᔮᕐᓇᖅᐸᒃᑐᖅ, ᐱᓗᐊᖅᑐᒥ ᖁᐸᓄᐊᖅᑕᖃᓂᕚᖕᒪᑦ ᐅᖃᓗᖃᐅᓯᓂᕚᖕᒪᑕ. “ᑎᐅ, ᑎᐅ, ᑎᐅ.”

We go camping in the spring. We spend all our time out with our cousins. These are good times, especially when the songbirds come back and sing their songs. “Tweet, tweet, tweet.”

ᐅᐱᕐᖔᒃᑯᑦ ᐃᓐᓇᐃᑦ ᖁᓚᖕᒋᖅᓯᓕᖅᐸᒃᑐᑦ. ᖁᓚᖕᒋᖅᓯᑎᑦᑐᒋᑦ, ᓂᐱᖃᖖᒋᑦᑎᐊᕆᐊᖃᓲᖑᔪᒍᑦ. ᓴᐃᓕᓇᓗᐊᒧᑦ ᖃᒧᑏᖕᓂ ᓯᓂᑦᑎᐊᕐᓇᖅᑐᖅ.
The grown-ups hunt for seals in the spring. While they wait for seals to come up for breath, we are told to be still and quiet. This is so relaxing that we fall asleep peacefully on the *qamutiik*.

ᓇᑦᑎᖅᑐᖃᕌᖓᑦ, ᒪᒪᕐᓂᖅᐹᒥᒃ ᓂᕆᑎᑕᐅᓲᖑᔪᒍᑦ. ᖃᕋᓴᖓᓂᒃ ᓂᕆᓪᓗᖓ ᐃᒪᐃᓕᓲᖑᔪᖓ, "ᓂᐋᒻ ᒪᒪᖅᑐᖅ!"
When a seal is caught, we are given the best part, the brain. It makes me go, "*Niam*! So delicious!"

ᖃᒧᒃᓯᖅᑐᑦ ᑕᐅᑐᒃᒍᒋᑦ ᐊᓂᐊᓇᐃᑦᑐᒻᒪᓈᑦ. ᑐᓰᑦᑐᒋᑦ ᖃᒧᒃᓯᖅᑐᑦ ᐃᒪᐃᓕᐅᖅᑎᑦᑐᒋᑦ. “ᐅᐊ-ᐄ! ᐆᐊ-ᐄ! ᐅᐊ-ᐄ!”

Watching a dog team run is so much fun. I love hearing the driver command the dogs. “*Ua ii*! *Ua ii*! *Ua ii*!”

ᐊᐅᔭᒃᑯᑦ, ᐸᒥᐅᔭᒦᓰᖑᔪᒍᑦ ᐃᒃᐱᐊᕐᔫᑉ ᑐᓄᑦᑎᐊᖓᓂ. ᒫᒃᑖᖅᑐᖅᐸᒃᑐᒍᑦ ᓄᑖᑦᑎᐊᓂᒃ. ᒪᒪᕐᓂᖅᐹᖑᖕᒥᔪᖅ. ᐊᓈᓇᒐ ᐊᒡᒍᐃᑦᑎᐊᒃᑳᓗᒃ ᒫᒃᑖᓂᒃ.
In the summer, we go camping around Pamiujaq, which is just north of Arctic Bay. We eat fresh *maktaaq*. It is so delicious. My mom is the best at cutting up the maktaaq.

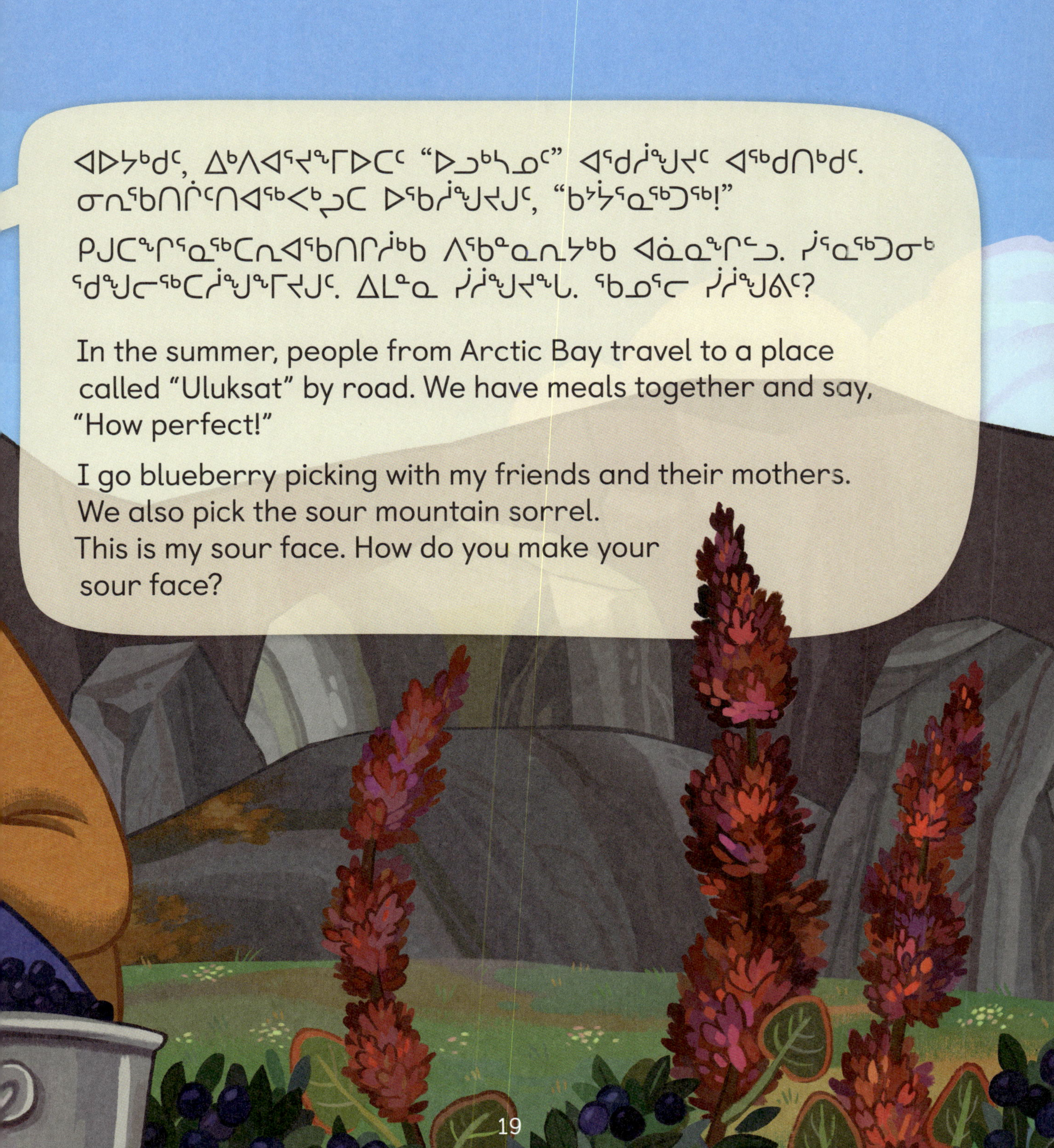

ᐊᐅᔭᒃᑯᑦ, ᐃᒃᐱᐊᕐᔪᖕᒥᐅᑕᑦ "ᐅᓗᒃᓴᓄᑦ" ᐊᕐᑯᓰᖕᒍᔪᑦ ᐊᖅᑯᑎᒃᑯᑦ.
ᓂᕆᖅᑕᑎᕇᑦᑎᐊᖅᐸᒃᑐᑕ ᐅᖃᓰᖕᒍᔪᒍᑦ, "ᑲᔾᔮᕐᓇᖅᑐᖅ!"

ᑭᒍᑕᖕᒥᕐᓇᖅᑕᓇᐊᖅᑲᑎᒥᓰᒃᑲ ᐱᖅᑲᓐᓇᓇᔭᒃᑲ ᐊᓈᓇᖕᒥᓪᓗ. ᓲᕐᓇᖅᑐᓂᒃ
ᖁᖕᒍᓕᖅᑕᓰᖕᒍᖕᒥᔪᒍᑦ. ᐃᒪᓐᓇ ᓯᓰᖕᒍᔪᖕᒐ. ᖃᓄᕐᓕ ᓯᓰᖕᒍᕕᑦ?

In the summer, people from Arctic Bay travel to a place called "Uluksat" by road. We have meals together and say, "How perfect!"

I go blueberry picking with my friends and their mothers. We also pick the sour mountain sorrel. This is my sour face. How do you make your sour face?

ᓯᒡᔭᒥ, ᐅᔭᖅᑲᓂᒃ ᓵᑦᑐᐱᐊᓂᒃ ᕿᓂᖅᓱᑕ ᐅᑦᑎᑲᐅᔭᖅᑎᑦᑎᓲᖑᔪᒍᑦ. ᖁᕕᐊᓇᖅᑐᖅ. ᓇᐅᔭᐃᑦ ᑐᓵᕙᒃᑕᕗᑦ ᖁᓕᑦᑎᒎᖅᑎᓪᓗᒋᑦ.
On the beach, we look for flat stones and make them skip on the water. It is a lot of fun. We hear seagulls flying overhead.

ᐊᐅᔭᒃᑯᑦ ᐱᔅᓯᑐᓖᖑᔪᒍᑦ. ᒪᒪᕐᓂᖅᐹᖑᓖᑦ.
ᐃᖃᓗᐃᑦ ᐃᒃᐱᑭᑦᑐᐊᕐᔪᖕᒦᙵᒑᖅᑐᑦ
ᒪᒪᕐᓂᖅᐹᖑᓖᖑᖕᒥᔪᑦ.
We eat *pissi* in the summer. It is so delicious. The char we catch at our fishing camp in Ikpikittuarjuk is also very delicious.

ᐊᐱᓕᕌᖓᑦ, ᓄᑖᖕᓂᒃ ᐃᓛᓐᓂᒃᑯᑦ ᑲᒥᒃᑖᓯᓰᖑᔪᖕᖓ,
ᖁᓕᑦᑕᐅᔭᒥᒃ, ᐅᕝᕙᓘᓐᓃᑦ ᐳᐊᓘᖕᓂᒃ, ᓇᓴᖅᒥᓪᓘᓐᓃᑦ.

ᖃᓐᓂᓕᕌᖓᑦ, ᐅᖃᓐᓄᑦ ᒥᐊᖅᓯᓇᓯᓰᖑᔪᖕᖓ. ᐃᒡᓚᕐᓇᖅᐸᒃᑐᓂ.
“ᒥᐊᖅ, ᒥᐊᖅ, ᒥᐊᖅ.”

When the snow comes back, I sometimes get new *kamiik*, a new parka, new mittens, or a new hat.

When the snow falls, I try to catch the snowflakes with my tongue. It makes me laugh. “*Miaq, miaq, miaq.*”

ᑖᖕᒋᓐᓇᓕᖅᑎᓪᓗᒍ, ᐊᖕᒋᕐᕋᑦᑎᓐᓂ ᐊᓕᐊᓇᐃᑦᑐᖅ.
ᓴᐃᓕᓇᖅᑐᖅ ᕐᑯᓪᓕᐅᑉ ᐃᑯᒪᖕᒐ ᑕᑯᓐᓈᖅᓱᒍ ᓯᓂᓐᓇᖅᓯᓕᕚᖕᒐᑦ.
When the skies become dark again, it is good to stay at home.
It is relaxing to watch the flickering flames of the *qulliq* at bedtime.

ᐃᒃᐱᐊᕐᔪᖕᒥᐅᑕᐅᓪᓗᓂ ᖁᕕᐊᓇᖅᑐᖅ ᑲᔾᔩᕐᓇᖅᓱᓂᓗ.
It is good to live in beautiful Arctic Bay.

Inuktut Glossary

Inuktut is the word for Inuit languages spoken in Canada, including Inuktitut and Inuinnaqtun. The pronunciation guides in this book are intended to support non-Inuktut speakers in their reading of Inuktut words. These pronunciations are not exact representations of how the words are pronounced by Inuktut speakers. For more resources on how to pronounce Inuktut words, visit inhabiteducation.com/inuitnipingit.

kamiik kah-MEEK	two skin boots
maktaaq mahk-TAHK	sliced narwhal or beluga skin, often with a bit of blubber attached
miaq MEE-ahk	an Inuktitut word used when a child wants to taste something
niam NI-am	yummy
pissi PIS-si	dried fish
qamutiik KAH-moo-teek	sled
qulliq KOO-leek	seal oil lamp
ua ii oo-AH-ee	an Inuktitut command used to get a dog team to run faster

ARVAAQ
PRESS